Plainsongs

Editor

Eric R. Tucker

Associate Editors

Becky Faber, Michael Catherwood, Eleanor Reeds

Editors Emeriti

Dwight Marsh, Laura Marvel-Wunderlich

Publisher

Corpus Callosum Press

Cover art by Chris Goedert

Corpus Callosum Press
Hastings, Nebraska

Subscriptions to *Plainsongs* are $25.00 annually for two issues, published in January and July. Subscriptions can be purchased online at the Corpus Callosum Press website.

Plainsongs welcomes submissions. The manuscript deadline for the Summer 2023 issue is December 15, 2022. Contributors will receive one free copy of the issue in which their poem appears. For each issue, the Board of Readers will select three poems to be honored as award poems. Award poem winners will receive a small monetary amount, currently $50.

Please use our online submission manager, available at the Corpus Callosum Press website, to submit work. Though we will endeavor to consider all e-mailed and snail-mailed submissions, we cannot guarantee responses for work submitted via these methods. Non-submission-related correspondence can be e-mailed to etucker@corpuscallosumpress.com or mailed to Corpus Callosum Press, PO Box 1563, Hastings, NE 68902. For more information about submitting poetry or subscribing to *Plainsongs*, please see our website: https://www.corpuscallosumpress.com/plainsongs.

Cover art by Chris Goedert.

Plainsongs is indexed by Humanities International Complete, EBSCO Information Services, 10 Estes Street, Ipswich, MA 01938.

ISBN-13 979-8-9853780-2-3

ISSN 1534-3820

Plainsongs

Winner of the Jane Geske Award,
presented by the Nebraska Center for the Book

Notes from the Editor

Thank you for picking up the summer 2022 issue of *Plainsongs* poetry journal. Within these pages, you'll find award-winning poems by Allisa Cherry, Roger Camp, and Todd Williams, accompanied by insightful essays written by associate editors Eleanor Reeds, Becky Faber, and Michael Catherwood. The issue also features an interview with Nebraska State Poet Matt Mason, whose new book *At the Corner of Fantasy and Main: Disneyland, Midlife and Churros* is now available; the interview begins on page 11. Mason and our associate editors were kind enough to contribute new poems to the issue as well. All told, the summer 2022 issue contains eighty-five new poems by talented poets from throughout the United States and around the world. Feel free to dive in anywhere. We hope you find much to enjoy inside.

We here at *Plainsongs* remain as excited as ever to be a venue for evocative, well-crafted, thought-provoking poems that run the stylistic gamut and that reflect the breadth of backgrounds, beliefs, identities, and ways of being that make up the human experience. There is beauty and strength in diversity, both on the page and in the world. Thank you for being part of our extended *Plainsongs* family. Be well, take care of one another, and have a joyful rest of the year.

Eric R. Tucker
Hastings, Nebraska

Contents

An Interview with Nebraska State Poet Matt Mason

Matt Mason began his term as Nebraska's State Poet in 2019. His fourth poetry collection, *At the Corner of Fantasy and Main: Disneyland, Midlife and Churros*, is now available. Mason's previous work includes *I Have a Poem the Size of the Moon* (2020), *The Baby That Ate Cincinnati* (2013), and *Things We Don't Know We Don't Know* (2006), which won a Nebraska Book Award.

Plainsongs: How have you and your family been holding up over the past two-plus years of the pandemic?

Matt Mason: That's hard to say…it's definitely been long. As a diabetic, I've tried to be doubly careful but also just looking out for others by acting responsibly. The first few months of the pandemic actually seemed good for my writing, but that quickly went the other way as my concentration seemed to get wonky. It's coming back, but it's been slow.

P: How has the pandemic affected the work you do as Nebraska's State Poet and as executive director of the Nebraska Writers Collective?

MM: It's definitely been a challenge as State Poet since my whole goal has been to do at least one poetry event in every one of Nebraska's ninety-three counties during my five-year term. I hit one-third of my goal in the first fourteen months, then the world shut down for two years. I'm slowly getting back going, but, well, slowly.

The Nebraska Writers Collective has been going well, actually. We pivoted quickly to providing online workshops in the summer of 2020, then moved our Louder Than a Bomb and Writers' Block programs online. We lost a few schools and correctional facilities, but not as many as I thought we would. We kept programs going, knowing they were even more important through this, that structured writing programs were huge help to a lot of people. And this year, we did the Louder Than a Bomb Festival in person for the first time since 2019, and we just selected Nebraska's second Youth Poet Laureate!

Another effect the pandemic likely had on my work life, though, is that I'm stepping down this summer as Executive Director of the Nebraska Writers Collective. My hope is to spend the last year and a half of my State Poet term doing more travel, more readings, more workshops. It's a test to see if I can make my living this way as, if I'm ever going to do that, it makes sense to try while I'm still the State Poet.

P: Can you say a bit about your creative process? How do you know when an idea or image will become a poem? Does the bulk of your writing tend to occur in a particular place or at a particular time of day?

MM: I have a weekly deadline to write a new poem, so I watch for ideas through the week to make sure I can start something by Monday night. And that's what the deadline does for me: it makes my writing more active as I'm not waiting for the poems, I'm searching for them. It seems the ideas or images that make a good poem come from the moments in a day when I find myself physically reacting to them. That can be a double take at something beautiful, disgust at a newspaper article, surprise at something a friend says, an overwhelming feeling I find myself cocking my head at, etc. This can happen any time of day, I just need to find someplace to sit by myself to draft out as much as I'm able. I used to be more of an after-dark writer, but having kids trained me to grab hold of an opportunity, no matter when that hit.

P: How would you describe the experience of writing and publishing your 2020 collection I Have a Poem the Size of the Moon? *Do you enjoy the process of putting a collection together?*

MM: I think putting a collection together is a blast; it's like writing a whole new poem where each poem for the collection is like a line in the overall work. It can be frustrating to find the right ones to include and then fretting over the order, but it's a similar creative feeling for me as writing a new poem.

I wanted *I Have a Poem the Size of the Moon* to be a book directly about Nebraska, so I looked through poems from as old as twenty-five years ago and made a pile to sort through and decide what would go together. I loved how an outer space theme also entered the equation and I'm excited by how the book turned out.

The only downer was that the book was set to debut in November of 2020, which, as you know, was a tough time to launch a book...

P: What's your earliest memory of reading and writing poetry?

MM: That would be writing weird things in elementary school when we did creative writing. I loved telling fantastic stories and making wild rhymes. Particularly ones about Santa Claus being hit by an airplane.

P: Who are some of your literary influences? Are there certain poets you find yourself going back to again and again?

MM: There are too many to list, as I'm indebted to so many writers. There are writers who I love reading and who I was lucky enough to meet and learn from like Galway Kinnell, Denise Duhamel, Patricia Smith, Bill Kloefkorn, Brenda Hillman, and Sharon Olds. Then there are the classics who opened up different areas of poetry for me, poets like John Keats, Robert Frost, Seamus Heaney, and so many others. Ask me again in ten minutes and I'll answer wildly differently as there are so many fantastic poets I have been inspired by.

P: What are some of the things you are working on right now?

MM: I'm working on very rough cuts of a few different possible manuscripts: one on eighties rock, one on road trips, one on my parents, one on the Old Testament, one on politics/the pandemic, and I'm always writing a new poem each week, which could open up something in a completely different direction.

P: Is there anything else you'd like to add?

MM: I have a poetry book that will hopefully be available by the time this interview is published. *At the Corner of Fantasy and Main: Disneyland, Midlife and Churros* was supposed to be released in April, but due to supply chain issues, the book has been on a boat from Korea that's bobbed offshore from LA for a month now. I hope it gets unloaded soon as I'm especially thrilled about this one. It's a little strange, but it's a lot of fun.

8 Beautiful Things (About This Last Year)

The way you used your car so little, the battery became a stone
that couldn't spark even a speck in the overhead when
you opened the door, couldn't make so much as a click
when you went to unlock the other doors with the switch.

The way you woke up
at 5am most mornings,
fully awake,
hoping there was good news.

The way, when the tree fell,
you cut a picnic
area from the emptiness
it cleared in your yard,
placed trunks and the widest
logs as stools, set yourself
there on summer afternoons
with a notebook and a cup of tea.

The way
cauliflower
is so surprising.

The way the dog smiles. The way he moves, room to room in the day:
to Sophia in Algebra class, to Lucia in Social Studies, you
in a flurry of emails and spreadsheets at the kitchen table,
your wife wrapping up teaching Composition to seventeen black
    squares on a computer screen;
you, ma'am, he says knowingly, need to get outside,
take a walk.

The way of these cookies,
the recipe Lucia has been working
to get perfect.

The way there is at last a truce between days:
where Monday is essentially just one more Thursday,
Sunday another sort of Wednesday, the autonomy
of Tuesday's declaration that it
is whatever it wishes to be.

The way of everything
you never imagined
you could miss
so much.

Matt Mason
Omaha, Nebraska

Stigmata

When I gave birth,
my mother
was there. Her distance,
too, was there.
Her ice-cold
permanent love, there,
a monolith of quiet.
The room agitated around me.
Every hot atom
ricocheted close
to my singular purpose.
But not my mother's atoms,
a perfection of stillness.
When she pinched my right palm
with her bloodless thumb
and index finger, she made
a cylinder of chill
that drove through me
like a nail and left a wound
I could push a life through.

Allisa Cherry
Portland, Oregon

About "Stigmata": A Plainsongs Award Poem

As the poem of my own composition included in this issue also reveals, I recently gave birth to my first child. My mother was not present for the delivery, except virtually, as my son was early and she lives an ocean away. Now she and I have matching zipper-like scars on our abdomens.

The relationship between a mother and a daughter is notoriously complex, never more so than when the daughter becomes a mother herself. Allisa Cherry narrates this transformative moment in "Stigmata" with the precision necessary to describe a deeply ambivalent relationship. The cliche of maternal frostiness is complicated by Cherry's language, which refuses to evaluate any quality that might adhere to a neat binary. The mother in this poem is an icy statue, defined initially by her "distance" as an innate characteristic rather than a relative condition between the two women, and yet this is what enables her to provide her daughter with the strength required to give birth. Her "stillness" in the midst of chaotic movement suits this "singular purpose" as the daughter is able to open her body without disintegrating.

The title of the poem and its concluding image of a nail-wounded palm invoke Jesus's crucifixion as a process akin to labor. Life can only be achieved through great pain and selfless sacrifice. I appreciate how Cherry appropriates the central figure for the mother in Western culture, the Virgin Mary, recalling her attendance at the bottom of the cross and the many images of the Pietà. In "Stigmata," however, a poem notably lacking in any masculine presence, the "bloodless" mother is more akin to the unreachable and draconian God the Father. The mother's love is "ice-cold / permanent" so, however paradoxically, a display of warmth would be counter to her daughter's certainty of such love's endurance.

Cherry crafts this poem so that it builds carefully to its core revelation. She establishes the jarringly aloof presence of the speaker's mother and then, in the poem's final and by far its longest sentence, describes the mother's apparent act of physical and emotional harm, only revealing it to be a gift in the last line. I think of the tiny red dots left at the base of my spine from being administered anesthetics during labor and delivery, and know a touch must often forego being gentle to be healing.

Eleanor Reeds
Hastings, Nebraska

I clumb more fences

than you've ever seen,
sputtered my father,
disentangling himself
from our laughter
and the barbwire
we splayed apart.
We were twelve, city boys,
hiking the rolling hills
sheltering the Russian River.

His boast bore truth,
a rancher's son,
he climbed a fence
every week-day morning
to mount Rags, his horse,
for the ride to school.

I learned two life lessons that day.

As a marine, traversing a field
of fire, I managed to crawl unsnagged
under concertina wire. More painfully,
that laughter can be barbed, too.

Roger Camp
Seal Beach, California

About "I clumb more fences":
A Plainsongs Award Poem

It's been a long time since I've heard someone talk about having "clumb" a fence. It's not unusual language for me; I was raised on a farm where barbwire (rather than the more formal term "barbed wire") was a common topic. I learned how to move both under and through it—lessons learned following multiple mishaps resulting in scars and torn clothing. Robert Frost said that "'Good fences make good neighbors,'" but the process of maneuvering fences can bring good lessons.

The poem opens with a strong—and grammatically nonstandard—statement of experience. In fluid and sparse lines, the poet brings together the players: young city boys who exhibit a lack of respect for a father whose life has been the opposite of theirs. The line "His boast bore truth" is the core of this poem. What follows in the second stanza gives us insight into the father: raised on a ranch, climbing fences since childhood, riding a horse to a country school.

The power of the poem comes in the single-line third stanza. In this line, the intent of the poet moves from descriptive to introspective. There is no preaching with that statement; the father is simply bearing truth. What follows in stanza four are two powerful and important lessons. The first, how being able to move under concertina wire (a type of barbwire formed in coils) enabled his ability to survive during his military service. The second lesson is a universal one: "that laughter can be barbed." The shame of laughing at one's father—the man who taught him about barbwire—is a heavy burden.

This poem is an excellent example of tight wording and intentional development. It speaks to truth.

Who gave you an important life lesson? Don't you owe that person a poem?

Becky Faber
Lincoln, Nebraska

The Cosmos

Little America, Devil's Tower,
and a thousand miles of two-way highway
filled windshields painted by insect remains
in the summer of our only family vacation,
so many hours spent squirming on leather seats
and listening to radio stations fade in
and out through a wind-bent antenna.

Roadside attractions remained our only redemption,
humbled outposts along forgotten trails
between Reno and Rushmore, their hand-painted signs
signalling to eager eyes to stop the car and see
the spectacular, world's biggest, most popular,
recently featured in *Ripley's Believe It or Not,*
a non-sequitur sequence of an America re-imagined.

Most memorable of all stood tall in the shadow
of the presidents themselves, a strongly skewed
collection of slanted shacks and wonders
of science called the Cosmos, a place for us four
to embrace in collective awe nature's laws
reversed, balls rolling up hills and unable to fall,
the majesty of mystery married to deception.

Photos remain the only evidence of our travels,
familiar people dressed in strange clothes smiling
sweetly back at cameras and posing for Polaroids
as some kind of proof of life we were family once,
finding our way back home one T-shirt shop at a time.

Todd Williams
Rapid City, South Dakota

About "The Cosmos":
A Plainsongs Award Poem

About subject matter, Flannery O'Connor wrote, "Anybody who has survived his childhood has enough information about life to last him the rest of his days." In Todd Williams's "The Cosmos," the poet weaves childhood vacation imagery of both the interior of the family car and exterior views from a trip that includes roadside attractions. Along the way, we learn bits of an Americana that still exists but is vanishing.

Williams uses a natural focus from inside the car, revealing "windshields painted by insect remains" and "hours spent squirming on leather seats." The family sits and listens to "radio stations fade in / and out through a wind-bent antenna." This crucial first stanza sets up the shift in the poem in the second stanza when the narrative reveals the world of "Roadside attractions." These "humbled outposts along forgotten trails" tell the story of a young boy and the excitement of discovery. Williams's descriptions weave through the poem and bring alive a young boy's imagination as he sees "hand-painted signs" that declare "world's biggest, most popular, / recently featured," all capturing the imagery of the trip.

The final turn begins when the family stops at "the Cosmos, a place for us four / to embrace…nature's laws / reversed." The final line of the third stanza sets up the last stanza: "the majesty of mystery married to deception."

The final stanza is heavy in understatement: "Photos remain the only evidence of our travels." Something has been lost, perhaps a simpler time, maybe more, but the second-to-last line carries enough emotion to quietly leave us wondering why the photographs are "some kind of proof of life we were family once," and the romantic vision of childhood seems blurry as a bug-smeared windshield.

Michael Catherwood
Omaha, Nebraska

Newborn

As he sighs into my breast, I trace
the asymmetric curve of a perfect ear,
tiny hairs of whitest down at its opening
and a lobe leant slightly back.
He has inherited our long eyelashes,
although the right one is crusted with yellow,
and the pale plumpness of his marshmallow arm,
the elbow creased like dough, the wrist dented
like a pillow, ends in a miniature fist of resistance.
Ever rounding cheeks and a blister on his top lip,
matching my unseen pair, make him look even more
like a hamster. His jaw trembles and squeezes
my flesh as I submit to a new compulsion:
to feed despite the pinch of pain and scabs,
the throbbing of blood and burning of nerves,
so that I melt away, become clear liquid,
then white, beading up on pink crevices.
This is a womanly art and I must invoke
old wisdom, kind mentors, summon the power
of silver, coconut oil, sheep's wool.
I was told this love affair needed only
ordinary devotion—I was told it was an act
of surrender and I try not to fight it as the hit,
the intoxicating shot, trembles through my body,
the body I gave of to grow him, the body
I am still giving of to the body my body made,
the pounds I gained now lost and I lose more
to fill him up with bulbous weights that beg him
not to sleep too long, not to stray too far,
for the everyday miracle of a new life
must be nurtured, must be adored
with love that is all action.

Eleanor Reeds
Hastings, Nebraska

Lost and Found

At first it was simply not seeing him,
a 10-year-old playing hide and seek—
so many places to disappear:
the barn, the chicken house, the granary.

Calling the boy's name, his father
searched,
looking around the yard
in the animal pens
throughout the tractor shed

but no sign

until, in the lowest desperation
that only a parent can feel,
he interrogated his other children
to find where they had last seen their brother.

Their answer: near the silo.

He raced to the top,
still a young man in his thirties,
looked down to see his son's arm sticking up
in a sea of gold.

Too late to save his boy
too broken to speak
too aware of how farm life devours children—
suffocating in a silo, crushed under a tractor when it rolls over,
broken by a fall from a haymow, mistakenly shot in a hunting
    accident.

Nothing stops on a farm—everything
has to keep going
so he did for another 60 years,
never spending a day without guilt and sorrow.

Becky Faber
Lincoln, Nebraska

Nebraska Highway 2

…you go down the river on the street to the sea!
   "Paso," Federico Garcia Lorca

Alive in high grass.
Alone in a slow river,
skin of a rotting stump.
The curl of smoke
clouds and settles
along a tight fence line.
Sunflowers bow and turn
their spines like whips.
Two towns away,
families hear the train
whistle gather,
the wind and land
like butterflies
on the brilliant dust
slipping away
slipping away
as a river runs
through a machinery
of silence.

Michael Catherwood
Omaha, Nebraska

oak maple

one oak one maple
planted four feet distant

while the oak grew up
patiently as expected
toward the noonday star

the maple bent to the west
a glint in the setting sun
drawing it away toward

black soil and leaves dripping
along the young dirt

this disorder upset
the farmer who tied ropes

to the maple yearning
to pull it back
to the east to the oak

toward its first steps
each guide staked like stone
chisels to the earth

each hand clutching
where they were not invited

two lives cannot help
where they find each day's sun

Corbett Buchly
Richardson, Texas

Fool the Sky to Cross the Sea

The monarch butterfly seems happy on
the butterfly bush. Purple flowers
sway, seaweed in the breeze.

\#

I am happy looking down on the monarch's
slowly beating wings. Not all bushes lead to
extinction. Not all eyes stare into a
mirror. Or a void.

\#

I saw a dragonfly rise 50 feet into
the air. I saw a dragonfly stand on a beach rose.

\#

I cracked abalone & tossed it to a seagull.
Who didn't understand.
Then ate the abalone.

\#

None of us have given a speech in front of parliament.
Accompanied Greta Thunberg on a voyage across
the Atlantic. The butterfly would be
the most skilled at this.

\#

A boy, I ran my fingertips across
the soft striped bodies of monarch caterpillars.
They were as common as little kids
who love caterpillars.

\#

When I go on a trip, I take
my existence in a backpack.
Ötzi the Iceman carried a leather
pouch that carried his life.

#

We are given an environment when we
incarnate & some of us know the law of
the land—how to climb up out of

the water on a reed, leave one
exoskeleton behind us as we puff out our new
sets of wings in the sun.

#

Some of us can anticipate where the fly
will be, not where the fly is now. Some of us
transform across the elements & some
of us forgot how.

Sam Cherubin
Norwalk, Connecticut

Thinking of a Friend

I never wanted to call you son.
The long winter came and the wind piled up
the snow and I wondered why I should
live alone in this cabin so far removed from
the way things are.

Nothing happens here.
Time and the island of pitiful summers
come and go without a word edgewise.
I want to remember you the way you were,
with your relentless hair and black
face shining like obsidian.

You have your reasons for leaving,
none of which involve me. I live one second
ahead of the real world and what the real
world thinks. I can never fathom the minds
of people who own their ideas of right
and wrong. My ideas are borrowed and never
returned.

I comb through bits of gravel
and pieces of the earth that have traveled here
from ages beyond recognition. I am someone's
forgotten amulet, left in a drawer for dusty years.
I find myself facing the sun. Without reason
I warm to the disputes that put me between
the pages of a book.

If you come as far as the river looking for me,
gaze into my windows to see if I still stir.
Walk up to my door and knock. There are people
I still like. There are ways to find me I've forgotten.

Joel Fry
Athens, Alabama

Yesterday I Worried About Money

It wasn't crimson on the cap of blackbird wings
or wound in knots of prairie grass.

It wasn't riding between dry coyote bones
or silt whirled up by mallard legs.

It was here. In the yard. In the house.
In the room. In the cupboards.

In what I ate and forgot to taste.

Swallowed forcefully, those invisible juices
that extract the sun from the rest.

Still it clung to the slippery walls of my throat,
where chickens carry rocks and glass.

Like all secrets, waiting in dusty corners to dart
when the door doesn't latch behind.

Giving chase through fields of ticks and rusting parts,
past where lungs can grab the air.

I should have let it out to run,
pant and tire, sleeping in the shed.

Instead it breaks apart, traveling
into places even I haven't been:

My spleen. My liver. My vertebra.
Behind my nose. The back of my eyes.

So small I allow it to stay.
So big I cannot force it to leave.

Linds Sanders
Missoula, Montana

Will it be over soon?

The bengal patrols the house.
He walks the wainscoting,
steps over and around
your mother's tchotchkes.
Over and over, around and around,
your mother stirs in her sleep.
The cancer goes unchecked by chemo,
green smoothies, experimental treatments.
She is dying. She cannot sleep restfully.
The hot flashes she originally
interpreted as menopause keep coming, over
and over, so she turns,
trying to escape them.
Your stepfather is passed out on the couch,
surrounded by the beer bottles
he drinks over and over, the green glass
one of the only constants
of your childhood.
And here we are in your childhood bed,
lined with the Lion King sheets.
Simba stares into me
as you push over and over,
as the creaking of the old mattress
stabs the night Simba stares
into me, I repeat your name quietly,
over and over your mother stirs in her bed
with a dream.

Callie S. Blackstone
Connecticut

Old Versifier Teaches a Community College Poetry Class

My mind isn't as sharp as it once was,
but it's smoother, slipperier, subtler.
It can teach how to survive being old.

You're not ready to learn that lesson.
Parsing poetry and emotional exegeses
of poems I love are dank, dark alleys.

We'll cover Whitman and Frost and
the hermetic lines published today
by holders of masters of fine arts,

but don't ask me to translate.
Elucidation of modern poetry
eludes my ability to enlighten.

This will be a waste of your time.
You'd learn as much about verse
if this class were taught by a mime.

I like rhyme. Don't ask me why.
I like meter. It lets me know
my thoughts are moving along

in some order or other, in some
human way that is not chaos,
for order is not free. Free verse

is unruly, naïve, thrashing about,
flexing its youth, and I am old.
I repeat myself. Or so I'm told.

You youngsters could teach me
a poetry my body used to know.
I have forgotten.

Rob Jacques
Bainbridge Island, Washington

We Christened That Abandoned House Ours,

the broken windows, faded graffiti,
bare bulbs. We read the writing

on the walls: *GA + JH forever*;
TONY LEE WAS HERE; *Welcome*

to Hell! We zipped our sleeping bags
together & found a safe space

to sleep: no sound of bottles
breaking, no broken glass

spanning the kitchen linoleum,
no knowledge of what would come

next: your father driving 50
on the peak's curves, going over

the cliff, & then me not knowing
what to say. This was back

before all that, before someone
bought the place & painted the door

blue. Before we broke things off
& went our separate ways.

I never knew what to say, only ached
for the last time I saw you:

you climbing out the window,
flashing a smile that said *I'll see you soon.*

Despy Boutris
Berkeley, California

The Children

The asylum schoolhouse is long-locked but not empty:
on a child-sized desk a tattered doll holds a tea party
with a glass vial labeled *laudanum*. It was compassionate
to teach children who lacked the innate capacity for reason,
those more bestial than the cowed prisoners led to expend
their animal passions in orderly gardens: now a wilderness
crowned with violet-red musk thistle, the outlaw cousins
of sunflowers said to choke cattle to death. Bindweed cracks
window glass, unfurling soundless white bells. Johnson grass
breaks past derelict floorboards, ascends the dirt-caked
classroom's sundried silence.

                             K describes
her old school desk, as though there is nothing remarkable
about growing up in the state asylum. Born in C Ward
to a silent reception among patients nodding like thistle
planted in metal chairs fused to brown floors, she never left.
From fellow students committed for idiocy or epilepsy,
she learned her first words. Tremulous scrawlings of horses
copied from picture books still adorn her open door. The farthest
she has traveled from the plastic mattress that has always
been hers is the graveyard beyond the quadruple set of doors.
Though the stones are marked only by numbers, she knows
which weights cover her childhood friends. I wonder if, like me,
she watches the bindweed climb and the yellow pigweed dig
deeper inside but dreams of poppies, ecstatic red chalices
bowing in a wind she cannot feel.

Lake Angela
Doylestown, Pennsylvania

The Fence

A week after your funeral, I went to the barn
To unload the truck. It was like Disney in there,
Swallows hanging straw garlands on the rafters,
Bunnies and chipmunks pressing their wet noses
Into my shins. We were supposed to build a fence
To keep them on their side of the property,
But we could never decide where to draw the line.
They did it for us: It took fourteen varmints
To carry one post to the mark the buck made
In the dirt, the first helpful thing he's done all year.
But the big surprise is that a possum can hold a drill.
My contribution was to tell them what to do,
As you had me: Sixteen fence panels, eighteen posts,
Chicken wire buried four inches deep to arrest
The burrowers. The only mistake we made
Was thinking no one but us could work the gate latch,
As if exiting, like entering, was something we could control.

M. H. Perry
Paris, Illinois

Amber Gazebo

The only thing I want to do is die alone
while the sun shines on the high seas
of imagination. I'm going to die haunted

by the moon's gentle soul. Of darkened
streets, I follow the absence of them, the way
they build their identity back to an absent

mother. I'm a cat with a lingering cold.
Left alone, I'm my own amber gazebo.
A starry night, too good to pass up, guides me

one creek at a time. At the mercy of the elements,
I flirt with enemies inside myself. I tap
a train window, looking for a new star

in the night. Ah, the innocent chain of children
changing the world restores me. If I had my way,
I'd face the belated remorse of my father despite

raindrops within our grasp. The sadness
of a lifetime steps up to my car again,
breaks my heart within its hands like earth.

The sound of Sunday's bells enters the maze
of me and finds a fall night when moonlight
seemed to flow lovingly over a gazebo.

Cliff Saunders
Myrtle Beach, South Carolina

A Great-Grandmother

We drive up the dirt road,
catching blue glimpses of East Bay.

By the shoulder a tree bends towards us
like a great-grandmother

almost kneeling,
guy-wires slack, branches spread low,

offering more sweet cherries
than we can pick: shiny dark.

      I saw her last July as we drove past.
      I thought she looked familiar then.

      I doubted
      she'd be here again.

      At the farmhouse
      my grandkids grabbed pails and ran

      to a row of younger trees,
      straighter and smoother.

This time I lead them back down
to her, our pails swinging.

William Palmer
Traverse City, Michigan

Central Standard

First snow. The red-winged blackbird laying tracks
outside our window sings the same song twice.
It's time for work. Time to rise, turn back
the blinking clocks like cursors and efface
what little light we saved—to double check
downed lines that overnight have stiffened, ice

a static on the screens through which the dark
extrudes as, bit by bit, the buffered dawn
is rendered slowly into suburbs, parks,
these potholed streets and pixelated lawns.
Next door a dog barks once. It's time for work.
For coffee and the long commute downtown

in weekend traffic, driving east past fields
that flicker ticker fast from row to row
of winter wheat, past stockyards, then the old
warehouses on the river. Time to sow
the roads again with salt before the cold
takes root in the concrete.—But first the snow

resumes, and, hardening on the window, rime
obscures each separate pane. The world goes white
with noise as plows on distant highways hum
us idled ones awake. It's time. A sleight
of blackbird disappears in ashes. Time
to leave this fall behind. To overwrite

all record of the morning yet to come.

Alison Talbott
Prairie Village, Kansas

Unfortunate Coincidence

One of you is lying.
    Dorothy Parker

Perhaps it is a coincidence,
the firestarter soot that tracks our every

footstep, the water sloshing
at every high tide into our four-

car garage. Perhaps it wasn't
our sunscreen that fouled

the coral. Or the smoke
from the jet on our trip

to show the new baby
to its Nana that settled

like sawdust between
the upturned eyes

of the flying squirrels.
Blame, I know, is a radio

whose frequencies are best
adjusted by the teeth

of coyotes. Soon, even the radios
will be floating, so much

jetsam in the bobbing
of the clear drink

of the still-spilling ice sheets.
We have had our ice cube

dispensers. Now the world
will find its toaster-oven way

to a suffering
that is indifferent

to culpability as much
as it is to our coming calamity.

Tom Daley
Cambridge, Massachusetts

October Meditation

even the dead are growing old
  Philip Levine

A line of Neruda
I will not recall again,
the ghostly call of the loon
over the vacant waters,
the least bittern
hidden in the reeds.
A woman to whom I am forgotten,
lips, breasts, thighs, bird-boned,
honey and salt and the sweet earth
I alone remember.
Old men ache for time and plenty.
Among the dunes exhausted waves
lunge for a weed-striped beach. Now
I walk a road that runs
like the tall white shadow of the moon
through blurred woods
lit by a slow black river,
and a valley of wind and bone,
below the haunted stars,
to the windswept, stony hills,
stark in the last light,
like the crooked spine of God.

Rick Rohdenburg
Duluth, Georgia

Heard at the Funeral

So, are you available in March? I'm getting married.
Your father was a good man. Where would you like the urn?
As usual, it's the pitching staff.

Do you have a pen that works? Mine quit.
They always play this.
What are y'all doing after the service?

Bow your heads please.
When we choose to love deeply, we also choose to grieve deeply.
He was cute, but I'm not ready for all that shit again.

That was some obituary.
I don't know how you do it. God must think you can handle it.
What is in that fucking jello?

Just can't believe it. Can. Not. Believe. It.
Have you seen Orange Is the New Black?
Totally worth it.

I hope people say nice things about me.
You make a killer guacamole.
Thanks.

Brian Builta
Arlington, Texas

The Puzzle

The teacups can cut your fingers
the obligatory relatives
the habits   oh the habits
you are hungry but
you don't like cooking smells
how the hell can I cook the food
without the smell?

It took me 38 years
to admit that
love is bondage
bondage and discipline.
If the above is true
your death so long ago
must have been a liberation
but oh the arms   voice   smile
what goes beyond
oh yes it was no liberation
oh yes it was loss
unadulterated loss
unconflicted   uncontested
unambivalent loss.

Loss   liberation
fit them together and
you solve the puzzle
you have the picture.

I put away
that jigsaw for more
than 38 years
now I put it together
right on the living room floor.

Iris Litt
Woodstock, New York

Infinite Sky

You should know where we are by now,
you've been looking at the map all day.
Haven't we traced these steps
a thousand times, salt on our skin,
dirt under our fingernails,
hoping to find our bearings?

You should know how to frame this—
press charcoal to paper,
sketch out a scene, add a soundtrack,
sell tickets. Forget the part
where we lose our way,
consider forgiveness instead.

You should know how it ends,
too—how the singer becomes the song,
how the river follows the road
for miles under an infinite sky
before it spills into the sea
in a reckless, joyous freedom.

Diana Donovan
Mill Valley, California

Dandelion Nights

Grass and flower beds speckled with yellow—
dandelions know no borders—the park, the
soccer field, yellow, yellow, polka-dot yellow,
round like the sun, shining like the sun, hot
yellow like the sun, jagged leaves un-matching
soft yellow centers. You can pop off the
yellow and dot yourself yellow. You can clip the leaves,
make salad. Overnight, puff balls zoom up, hot air
balloons of seeds parachuting on invisible breezes,
long spindly stems reaching toward the ancestor
sun remembered in chlorophyll green, but really,
dandelion puffs, don't you know, it's the moon
you want, the dark carpet of night with the reflection
of spherical purity bitten off in parts by shadow and wind.

Wendy BooydeGraaff
Kentwood, Michigan

Something Like This

<u>Waldeinzamkeit</u> – (*German*. vol-TINE-zom-kite) She has broken off the engagement for the third and final time. You know it really is over because she took the sourdough starter when she left. Your hand was on your mother's heart when she died. You cannot get disability, and they have just closed the only decent bookstore in your town. Now you are walking along a tall mountain ridge among red oaks. They are vastly older than you, and they lean toward you sympathetically. Or, they are laughing. Either is fine with you.

J. Stephen Rhodes
Charleston, South Carolina

Very Like a Whale

No, he's definitely a whale, plunging
up the coast toward Santa Barbara
going my way, lifting and crashing.
He must be the last word in leviathans.
And it's almost like he has an eye
on me, making this a race to Monterrey.

He pulls an ocean behind him—
that impossible and polished expanse.
He lunges and plummets, the great head
versus half a planet of these waters.
He pummels them, a prize fighter,
indefatigable, victory in his pulse.

When my head turns, he's still there;
to all appearances there is intent.
I know he's not a kindred spirit, only
the most impressive mammal on offer.
Our directions are the same for now.
The proportions of the coincidence amaze.

It's a conceit that makes me think
he takes notice of me at all.
I'm not being shadowed; we won't share
the same diner. He's not coming or going;
home is where he is and that water is all
his world. There's no itinerary in him.

The road departs the coast for a mile;
when it's back the sea is smooth of him.
He's gone deep, farther than the living
ought, part of the unappeasable motion,
a telling gesture of the sea,
that brawn of water very like a whale.

Todd Johnson
Racine, Wisconsin

The Significance of Touch

Perhaps you have noticed
how the lightest touch
provides balance
takes away the fear that you are falling.
Shoulder against doorframe
tugging on your stocking.
A few fingers lightly on the barre
not even supporting the dancer's arch.
The eyes' quick brush of the horizon
lending confidence you are here
firm between earth and heaven.

Or noticed how someone's palm
cupping your shoulder briefly
or laid across the small of your back
orients you in the order of things.
Even the scent of another hand
that has shaken yours
arresting the drop into loneliness.

You are not about to fall
the way things do
the way tipped from the pan
the washing-water carries the peccable grains
back to the ground
while you rise rinsed immaculate
to the banquet
four fingers nestled
in the elbow of the host
touched
taking your place
on the fulcrum
between now and then.

Jennifer M. Phillips
Barnstable, Massachusetts

Still Waters Run

deep is what you expect to hear,
suggestion of wisdom and profound
thoughts beneath the silence

from someone who pays attention,
listens more than talks. When
my mother said this of my father

she meant he was devious, unknown,
deep into himself, hiding what she
feared to know. He thought of himself

as deep, I'm sure, thought his writing
beautiful and eloquent. I will tell you
now, he was a small and shallow man,

not a reader or thinker, without political
knowledge or opinions. He collected
coins and stamps, expressed no artistic

leanings or appreciation. From childhood,
he hoarded quarters, didn't share. He lied

as a way to be secretive, kept feelings
in his gut, hid money from the IRS
and us. Inside, he roiled and suffered,

confused and flustered. He couldn't
cope with a rainy day.
I never saw his depth.

Joan Mazza
Mineral, Virginia

The Paint Rep of Erie

I misrepresent my
self
saying I sell paint for
a living
always on the road that circles the fine edges of Lake Erie
like a strip of blue tape unrolled and stuck down to mask off
    beginnings from ends
clean lines that divide the water from the seawalls and sand.

I am maybe at best a wanderer
through shoreline motels and perch cafes
calling on accounts every primary day
big hardware stores that carry my name
in metal cans that once were cars
the crushed-up scrap of what remains
after you've driven them over pot-holed bridges
and scrape up against guard rails along the harbor curves.

I peel off the tape every all-you-can-eat night
in one, long, tacky, circumference pull
resetting the margins of tomorrow's existence
in the vacancy must of a stained room single
with a death pile bed spread
and moon cloak drapes
then iron a fresh shirt with a stirrable logo
in case there is such a thing as the right shade
in the blinking light of brush and stick
for love to be rebated.

On Tuesday I'll have coffee with the paint manager who mixes in
    creamer from a jar
and buy muffins for the sales crew who wear short, white aprons
    and splatter me on their shoes.

Ken Been
West Bloomfield, Michigan

everyone here is out to get me

ego didn't let me run for the bus, so I
let 79 go by and waited for 28. the
bench was wet with cold. an old
man stared me down until I grimaced
myself out of my seat. I wasn't being facetious
trying to hold my spot—my achilles'
tendon had been inflamed from
dodging dog shit on my daily nightly
lonely walks. I leaned against the stile
with the sun cutting my eyes. I wondered
how many honks on the street were for me,
calls to tell me I looked wonderfully
alone in the city. I thought about when
someone would text me back and take
me up on offers for coffee dished out
months ago. I wondered still when
the bus would come. always late.
I remembered my first week here,
the first time I rode bus 28 and how
it slid on ice and toppled. red beast
marked and fallen. the man standing
next to me fell, too. we both reached
for the emergency hammer to crack
a window and let the air in. steam from
the malfunctioning exit warmed
my face. my cheeks were cherries
on a gaunt white plate, something the local girls
loved to pick and kiss before leaving
the fruit to sweet itself dry.
evacuees vacated the bus
after the man opened it wide. *Will you
come follow us?* he asked. *If you stay
too long at the scene of an accident,
you'll have a year of bad luck.*

I laughed at what he said, but I realize
now I did not make it out of the bus
in time.

Ajla Dizdarević
Paris, France

Why I Get Anxious Crossing the Street

I've been afraid that if she could fall
like that, so could I, so could everyone
I love, so could every person I see
on the street, all of us. I've felt

like a bird without feathers crossing
Wilshire Boulevard, in danger driving
down quiet back roads, walking up steps,
stepping on the flat sidewalk. Everywhere

it seems there are reminders, a sign
in LA, Franklin, the name of her street
in New York. A homeless woman
in the alley yesterday stooped to look

at her belongings, plastic grocery bags
filled with things, like she was evaluating
what to keep, what to ditch, just as I've
bent in front of my closet deciding

what to keep, what to ditch. Still, no one
told me this would happen, that something
terrible will happen. So, I'm telling you.
And I am sorry. And you're welcome.

Cynthia Good
Atlanta, Georgia

Midsummer

Hurricane Barry eases onto the landscape
wearing cargo shorts and carrying a cooler,
intent on staying awhile. "Does being busy
make death more bearable?"
he asks after his fifth Fat Tire.

We resign ourselves to days of rain.
The frogs croak hallelujah.
Tonight could be like the rest, lost

in the planning of what's next.
Instead, I lie down beside my baby,
refuse all I've left undone.

Paulette Guerin
Searcy, Arkansas

Hanging Out with Frida Kahlo Between the Roots and the Scree

after Frida Kahlo's "El Predregal," 1943

She reclines
in a hardscrabble landscape—
her elbow cradled on a pillow—
brief comfort among sharp stones.

She hides
under the orange of a skirt
that says *calla lily*
that says *brusmangia*
that says *esperanza jubilee.*

Oh! but the vines—
broad leafed and blood veined—
rustle and reach
through a window
in Frida's torso
where her heart should be.

I shout:
There is a hole where your heart should be!
Even the stones show through!
I touch her all over her wound.   I ask how.   I ask why.
My hands bat at the vines.   I want to see what is missing.

But Frida only watches—
her arm stretched along her side—
her hand resting just there—
all quiet but the roaring of her eyes.

Jennifer Filardo
St. Paul, Minnesota

Rebuilding What Remains

to my brother Bruce

Thoughts of a hemi engine block
vaulted chapels empty

of carburetors, pistons, timing chains
interred in salvage yards

a torque wrench, bereft
of its ticking, tightening advance.

Things never understood
scattered over pages, slight

as a ripple of air displaced
one fleeting afternoon

at the Mineral County airport
its runway become a drag strip

two stock cars straining
the Christmas tree goes green

and on screaming smoking feet
four hundred twenty five horses

carry you down
your quarter-mile journey.

I lay them out. Piece them together.
Run what I've rebuilt, again

each finish only a start.

Mike Barrett
Seattle, Washington

Abandoned Nests

Summertime's trees held many songs
the vocalists were guests of course

Gazing up into branches holding green
I will sometimes see one blot
of nest forsaken now like a cellar hole
sunk in underbrush the nestlings

fledged or eaten parents flown or fallen
nothing new there under the sun
here in New Hampshire where we have
in our woods whole abandoned towns

An old nest may fall from its limb
for a child to pick up and carry home
if her elders will have it or to school
for show-and-tell or an older child

for a science project the wise teacher
will tell the class how it was woven
how cowbirds lay their eggs in nests
of other birds for other birds to raise

a light goes on and one little scholar
toward the back waves a hand
and tells the class That's what happened
to me and my sister we're adopted

Teacher explains how broken eggshells
under a tree could mean anything

Russell Rowland
Meredith, New Hampshire

Dolason Prairie to Emerald Creek— and Back

I went to the woods alone and hiked all day in the solitude
of my thoughts: a mass of mosquitoes

buzzing about my head; at once
everywhere and nowhere. I hiked on past what remains

of the old sheep barn across the meadow and into shady invitation
    of the madrones
and bays. In the coolness, my thoughts fell away. Only

my body kept the rhythm of my steps. I dropped the worries:
clothes, hands, feet, body, bones. I crossed

another section of prairie, then the shadows
of the great redwoods swallowed what remained. I breathed

in the scent of the sword and maidenhair ferns,
the sorrel at my feet. I started

again: this time only soul arriving at Emerald Creek. There
in the stillness I rested and plucked a stone from the creek,

thought of the shape of one's life, its heft and polish. I placed it
    back
into the waters where it might be worn to nothing. Rose

up in the long, hot afternoon, stepping back into breath, putting
on a new suit of skin and bones to bear me home.

David Holper
Eureka, California

Mesothelioma Sestina

They said it wouldn't burn.
But we could feel it like a blanket
smothering us from the inside/out.
They said it was safe.
It wasn't enough to just send us to gather it in the mine,
every day we brought more up, in our breath.

Men stacked fish-deep in an elevator, sucking shallow breath—
worried their dark thoughts will ignite and burn.
The weight of the darkness like a blanket
in your pockets, wearing out
two holes where your hands hid—safe
from your shaking eyes, as you shuffle into your shift, their mine.

That's a funny thought. That it's *mine*,
not theirs. But your breath
is only yours. Like a match you burn
against the cup of your hand, an old blanket
of stars—familiar as a thumbprint. Set out
to find something new, and you'll lose what's safe.

That's what she says every time you're home safe.
"Praise God, and let the devil know you're mine."
You can feel her hot breath
on your neck as you sleep, as your thoughts burn
against the light, like moths birthed when you fold the blanket,
try to set things right in a square, smooth them out

and make something better than what sifts out
of the rail cars, into what sits dusty in a safe.
You can tell them at the mine
about your children, their sweet breath
whistling as you inhale every day like a burn
across your lungs, a blanket

over your chest. Time weighs like a rotting blanket
and stones you can't piss out.
It holds you down with the irony that it keeps others safe

(but not from dust you dig from the mine).
It wasn't your windows fogged with winter breath
but your lungs that will slowly frost and then burn.

They sold your breath in the mine,
abandoned you like a babe in a blanket and called it safe.
The doctors cannot take it out. You can only sit and burn.

Anne Holub
Billings, Montana

The Burial

Along the outskirts of my old school,
beyond the shade of blackjack oaks
and the hard acorn hills of fescue grass,

a footpath leads to the landfill,
the small-town shrine to bygone birthdays
and castaway Christmas mornings.

And here is where my father stood,
the old cedarwood of my governance,
when he clicked the car hatch open,

tossing the hauls to the wind.
All of my childhood myths and toys
bulldozed in the landfill:

a Spyder bike—a single-seater—
swallowed by the rain. A Scuba Joe
in diving gear; a tin-plate model train.

Deep in the sunless red clay dirt,
pale roots of young trees
push the flanks of plastic men,

turning the guns as I once did,
arms and legs—the bayonets—locked
in a never-ending battle.

For over fifty years, mimosa branches
have arched over the muddy ground,
forming a headstone,

splintering the noonday sun
into fractals of starlike shapes,
illuminating dust motes and pollen

suspended in long shafts of yellow light,
the remnants of my father's flame,
burnished and gold.

Keith Gorman
Alcoa, Tennessee

The Birdwatcher

after a photo by Matej Sefcik

In Central Park, birds act as brusque and impatient
as any New Yorker. The woman stands there, her hands
holding binoculars to hopeful eyes, eager to catch
sight of a tufted titmouse or common yellowthroat.
She's seen them before, of course, who hasn't,
but she loves the way they flit on branches,
how huffy they seem, blaring pissed-off vibes
in a fracas of tweets so blue her grandmother would blush.

She doesn't take their pique personally—after all,
you can't survive in the City if your feelings bruise
like dropped fruit at a bodega. Today though,
her binoculars disappoint. The only wildlife she notices
are the harassed New Yorkers in their native habitat.
If she looks hard enough, she can almost see their exotic plumes.

JC Reilly
Marietta, Georgia

A Keepsake

"What would it take,"

my father penned
on the note we found
among my mother's things,

"for you to remember
to shut this door and
turn off the light?"

I wondered why
he chose to leave a note—
though she always was a reader—

and why she'd saved
this yellowed square
with brittle tape along one edge.

Steve Nielsen
Omaha, Nebraska

Funeral

The marigolds are indiscriminate,
a profusion plying roadside
and garden alike. They take no notice.
The sky is perfect blue,
cerulean joy demanding more
than its share of the scene.
The mother is a wooden toy,
her arms stretched into straight pins
as she falls against the coffin,
her head bent back,
her gaunt face exposed.
She would have the sky take her,
carry her away in mare's tail clouds,
a gauze of torn strips.

Yvonne Pearson
Minneapolis, Minnesota

The Gift

Imagine the aftermath
water a continuous stream

the surface unshattered
dignity as simple

there won't be a letter
Death of Marat like

a painter's conceit
let platitudes drown

death might be a chair
the hand grasps neither

a tantrum how irresponsible
how cruel they will say

we paint in brightness
sculpt they demand

their eyes are museumed
your artistry is theater

to conjure height so tall
divine a grand symmetry

so steal the heirloom watch
to absolve forgive freely

there might be a bathtub
no, better to be placid

faucets fingertip damp
as not falling off a toilet

too gloomy inspiring staged
every fabric fold perfect

pale face shadowed
in steamy vats

lacking sides or cushion
quill nor paper

they might insist
thoughtless what about us

ours are waves of Pantone
your clay into risible shapes

while you molded the sky
oh the gift

as to be invisible
know what is behind the air

then confess show them how
even when no one asks.

Rachel R. Baum
Saratoga Springs, New York

Loss of a More Aquatic Nature

Every son has a father   the Titanic sinking   deep in his arms
    the sea   a bruised   shoreline of kisses

your head on a bed   the length of his body
    awake & waiting   for an angel's arrival

to visit him   in the shape of gone
    making you a ghost   the mirror finds pretty

on the bedroom wall   in a black & white film
    as the violin's horsehair   strokes the sky

and the last ounce of steel   makes Ireland sad   for screws
    that turned for this   as sharks fed on prayers

of repentance   water churned with champagne   and bones
    that's when I poured   the sea in a glass

that's when he said   I looked   like a cork
    his little hand   could hold   on to.

Daniel Edward Moore
Oak Harbor, Washington

Swarm

Clinging to my hair,
little breathing barrettes.

Forceful kicks, small
razor-barbed feet.

Bodies the size of a half-
smoked cig, spitting brown

tobacco-type juice when
trapped between palms.

Legs rubbing toothlike
ridges on wings—buzzing,

stirring the meadows
between hums and leaps.

These locusts binge
on grasses and wheats:

Harmless as one,
ravenous as many.

Tiny things will
eat eat eat eat eat

until the grasses
no longer move
for you or me.

Holly Dodge
North Mankato, Minnesota

I should get a macro lens. But no.

I seek
the intimacy of
soft edges,
blurred focus,
undefined borders.

I am not interested in scrutiny,
nor in defining things
as clearly as they can be perceived
outside of human perception.
I accept and embrace that limitation.

I do not want to discuss
the difference in semantics and meaning
between "sympathy" and "empathy."
Especially not when all I need
is a hug and a shoulder to cry on.

I do not need
the newest technology,
the latest trend,
crispness in focus
in fashion…or being…

I just want the human connection
in conveying what I see
in the world
in ways that I know
are not solely my own.

An expression and conversation
of pure thoughts,
not a precise, concise articulation
of specified interpretations.
Only what I know as here and now.

The accessibility of the intangible,
left to its own devices,
is my justification.
I needn't apologize for myself,
I have nothing more to prove.

I have nothing more to say.

Jennifer Weigel
McPherson, Kansas

Voyeurism

A poet looks at the world as a man looks at a woman.
  Wallace Stevens

It's not what you think. It's something else
which can only be had by waiting. Until
you see surrounding hills and meadows wrinkle
and bunch, then begin to undulate, heaving out
haunches, flanks, thighs and torsos
with limbs in all the postures of love.

It's arousing, yes, but not what you think.
The shoulders of a bull can make me burn.
and the look of the fox I surprise near my door
smolders in me a long time after.
Even nude winter trees take root in me,
their haunted limbs stretching pointedly.

It's arousing but I stand apart,
as full of watching as the star of life,
present but unnoticed, persistent, hot.
With my eyes undressing and penetrating,
I taste the honey without having to eat,
from a distance, waiting, spilling over.

What need is there to touch or possess?
I know where all are tending. Hear trees
being sawed up, and coffins building,
cracks opening in concrete foundations.
The wind is the messenger. The breath, fire.
There is no need to possess.

Mark Christhilf
Nutley, New Jersey

on removing foreign flesh from your body

afterwards, you relish the idea of
being cut open, skin flayed and
extirpated, glands and adipocere
transformed into ash, that
holy transcendence into smoke, body
of incense and intercedence to the
gods, confession and penance—
the lashings of a scalpel against your
skin, the forgiveness that comes
in sutures, the sacrament of
laying yourself down before the
bright lights and masked faces, a
thousand silent prayers that you
wake up in time to love this body
you have created for yourself,
unholy and broken,
finally yours

Eliot Claire
Chicago, Illinois

You'll Want Kids Someday

If my womb were a house,
it wouldn't have neat shutters
and a manicured lawn.
No wide front porch
with out-facing welcome mat
in front of a door that's never locked.

No one enters my womb
to find cookies in the oven
or a pie on the windowsill.

My womb is ramshackle.

A tilting affair with cracks
in the sidewalk and broken
fence pickets mended
with sheet metal and wire.

Where children sprint past,
holding their breath,
making the sign of the cross.

My womb's door has five deadbolts
and an ill-tempered guard dog
with filed teeth and a barbed wire collar.

Politicians and friends of Jehovah
skip my womb like homeroom,

tossing flyers and sodden copies of
The Watchtower onto the pile
drifted against the gate.

Once a month, the neighbors
on either side
send care packages, hoping
a nice family will move in
and improve their property values.

My womb holds them,
unopened, for a week,
fuming at the presumption,
before sneaking them into the bins
at night to be collected by sanitation.

I wish I could sell it,
this ever-vacant house,
to someone who
would fill it with children,
plant pansies in the garden:
the things my mother-in-law
says I should do.

Instead, I exist under its weight
and the side-eyed stares of neighborhood women
who have no room in their imaginations

for the freedom of vacancy,
the love of things never born.

Traci McMickle
Great Falls, Montana

Bookstore

It was like we opened a bookstore.

We painted the walls "Nautical Blue,"
You sanded the floors while I
Stained the counter which holds the antique
register that goes -Ching!-
We constructed strong shelves of cedar and
Categorized aisles with eccentricity:
"Probable Nonfiction," "Tall Tales (And Short Ones),"
"Historical Romance for the Single Ladies,"
"Cookbooks If You Dare, But Don't Blame Us."

On opening day, hope everywhere,
We stood in the doorway,
You in your overalls and me with a
Bandana over my hair, and welcomed
Fresh breeze and a flurry of customers inside,
But when they entered—surprised—
To see no books (shelves bare), we
Reminded them we never
Actually promised them anything
And began to tell them stories.

A soap-opera-style parody of a
Dysfunctional Thanksgiving dinner.
A murder mystery, but the reader did it.
(It was you.)
The death of the coral reef
And everything inside it.
The birth of the last litter of thylacines (maybe).
The tragic history of the pickling industry.
And they laughed, and they cried, and
They were riveted, and heartbroken, and
Disappointed, just like they ought to be,
And then we turned out the lights.

It was all just so fucking empty, it was.
But it was like we opened a bookstore,
Except we didn't.

Bridget Spoerri
Milwaukee, Wisconsin

Measuring Pain

A friend's story of measurement stays with me.
A woman bringing fevered child to doctor,
into that white clinic's glare,
reporting, in reply to routine questions,
that the child's heat came to
three hundred fifty degrees.
One pictures the doctor's raised eyebrows,
cynical readiness to disdain the mother.
How, he asked, had she determined this?

She placed one hand on the child's chest,
the other in the oven, gradually warming.
When her oven hand and hand on child felt equal
she knew the measure of her child's heat.
For the doctor, an anecdote.
The child, administered an antibiotic, goes home.
The mother disappears into story.

Where can I place my palm
to measure my still-awakening anger?
How it rises when memory brings back
my now dead husband's lies and ridicule.
Would it do to put my hand on a woman
deported back to Mexico?
On the forehead of a Palestinian
searching his destroyed home?
On the arm of that woman beaten
to the pavement at a BLM demonstration?
No. You raise your eyebrows.
Their heat surely surpasses mine.
You say I exaggerate.
Tell me I'll forget this antique fury.
I will never forget.
I will never forgive.
But perhaps in time, perhaps the fever will subside,
memories dimming, drifting back, cooling.

Put your hand on my head, hold me.
You take the measure of this pain.
You tell me.

Anne Bower
South Pomfret, Vermont

brutal all night

somehow you got the cops to buy you a motel room
when they kicked you out of another vacant lot,
so my brown jacket was sagging off the edge of a motel bed this
    morning
while outside on our side of the fence a struggling tattoo artist
walked his brown oregonian dog up and down
the parking lot,
his head shaved,
he was looking for work
or a smoke to save for later.
when we met him he asked if we were rolling
and got a cigarette out of us
and you told him he could find canvas down by the levee.

and i'm not sure, but sometimes i think all this is a bit like loving
the electric foxtrot of modern times. what i mean
is, i have no good reasons for the things i do. that is to say,
it's hard to love on purpose.
but for all that, i can't help myself
if at times i fall back to your groove.

i think it's how you tucked the tag back into my sweater.
i think it's how you took pains to dent the minifridge with a
    basketball.
i think it's how you held my face and thanked me for bringing you
    bandages at 4am,
and how when we got back first thing after sunrise to find a woman
    at the flap of your tent
mooning us and shouting the most precise
and meaningless things to do with hans zimmer and the santa cruz
    city government
you and your lankiest friend introduced me.
i think it's how you shout at cops.
i think it's how you walk through fog.

i think it's how you walked
with your longboard, your backpack, your basketball, and your sun
    hat
through the fog.

Emi Lohman
Olympia, Washington

Jumper Cables

On top a spare tire
tucked beneath the truck's false bed,
so when time came
to bring the dead back to life,
we'd be ready and able,
but I fear we never learned how.

And though it never died,
it steadily ground its way down
until the miles and years wore it rusty—
I emptied the trunk to resell and found
those dusty black and red cables we kept,

    still unsure how to connect.

Aaron Sandberg
Schaumburg, Illinois

In the Service Industry

Sometimes I'll curl up and sleep
on my work table, a benefit of being small.
The dreams I have there deserve me.

A wooden table like ones at L'Auberge
where I rubbed down the shakers,
I married the catsups as our sous chef unwrapped thick loins.

My bartender, his name was Turtle, called
me over and said see that reserved sign?
Every Sunday a large human man

comes in and orders two fixed prix meals
and eats the whole thing by himself.
I'd marry this man, he said.

We stood at the top of the stairs, royals
of the court of rooms before rush. Cutlery
set for the fists of the movers and shakers.

Asleep on my table, in my suspension,
I'm caught between "consistency and disarray"
My mind goes through the settings,

how a candle, snuffed,
still holds a line to the burning sunset,
moving so easily from threat to memorial.

Merridawn Duckler
Portland, Oregon

Forty Years

We foundered in and out of love,
hated one another, buttered toast,
raised three children,
lost two fathers, got a new knee,
fused two vertebrae, in sickness
lying mostly alone sometimes
together, watched concussion
come and go, the dilated pupil
of our son's eye lit at night
by your flashlight,
the first daughter's marriage
a fete of magnificent proportions,
the second daughter's quick one
in the courtroom
shortly before our third grandchild.
Our forty years came and went
through grounds fragrant
with lilac and wisteria
even though one summer
when a tree fell flat over with a loud crack
for no reason either of us
could fathom you came up
with a scientific explanation.

Judith Skillman
Newcastle, Washington

Telling the Truth

I called my mother up yesterday
inviting her over to this side:
she forever 69; I sidling toward 75.

She took a seat in the Adirondack chair
next to mine, looked me in the eye and listened
as I told her, for the first time, truth.

I said I could not carry any farther her stones
of guilt, the knots of loss she had left,
I thought, for me to carry on.

The stones were growing older, heavier.
The knots grew tighter because
I had no free hands to untangle them.

That was it. That was all I had to say.
She listened, nodded, the sun
glinting on her glasses. Finally

we turned from each other at precisely
the same moment, swung our heads like cows
to gaze across the prairie to the hills.

Kathleen A. Dale
Milwaukee, Wisconsin

Theaters of the Absurd

Your temper flares like natural gas.
The morning recoils in horror,
scattering our last few songbirds.

The dim face with which I awoke
won't last me until lunchtime.
Can't you curb your anger

at the world and allow me
a moment of casual pastels?
I know the political moment

overlaps the personal angst
with a rustle of seaweed torn
from the cringing ocean floor.

I know the most infamous crimes
have already been claimed by others
for their theaters of the absurd.

Let's settle for coffee and scones
by the river. Maybe the heave
and sigh of heat will nurse us

back to the poignant lassitude
we discovered in each other
in our years of leather and chains.

Or did we see that on TV,
some British program devoted
to poets no one ever reads?

Let's avoid scraping our flesh
on each other's sharpened edge.
Your temper burns so brightly

that for a moment I can read
bedrock so far underground
that its hieroglyphs seem human.

William Doreski
Peterborough, New Hampshire

Waiting on the Quays, Twenty Years Ago

It felt light between my lips
barely there really
I sucked
took the smoke into my mouth
held it there, waited
for what I thought
was the right amount of time
before I exhaled
the smoke hanging between us
on the cold winter air

he smiled, laughed a little
explained that I had to take it in
take it down
into my lungs
that I should concentrate
on making the smoke
come from my nostrils

he showed me
it looked easy
I tried again
tried to swallow the smoke
but I could not
for whatever reason

he said that I was better off
that it was a nasty
and expensive habit
I told him that I wanted to try it
to get it right once
at least

he shrugged his shoulders
the last bus on the horizon
taking him to Bray
me, to Kildare
we stood on the quays

him, smoking his cigarette
me, just watching mine burn out
I cupped my hands around it
expecting heat
there was none

Steve Denehan
Naas, County Kildare, Ireland

Calendar Girl—April

Spring is a fading map of winter.
As the sun strips ice from fields,

she exhales. It's time to put down
her hair, put on her bracelets,

and spin and spin and spin
on the new lawn carpeting up

spiky between her toes,
and smelling like a world reborn.

It's all about the boots and music,
Saturday night dances springing up

from here to across the border,
honky tonks, jukeboxes and radios all night,

a wealth of warmth falling on bare shoulders
all day. A balmy breeze. A hardblue sky.

Sundress stained with the beginnings of flowers
and luminous fragments of joy touch everyone.

She drinks in the colors, pure and sweet,
packs away the winter beiges and grays,

digs out her sandals, follows the sounds
of water over river stones, the rush of wings.

Tobi Alfier
Torrance, California

Migration

before I shut the door
        I hear your cries
my eyes arrested as
        indistinct and far away
you spread like grass seeds
        across the plane of sky
moving south

Should I run inside and grab my camera
the lense would not be wide enough to catch the entire sky

most days I forget to dream of leaving
why leave if I have no where else to go?
but seeing you up there is drug enough to shake my
certainty

Normal people don't just up and leave.
They make plans and schedule flights and book hotels.
They pack suitcases.
They make arrangements.

still as I watch
        your straggled lines advance
        like camels in the desert blue
I long to follow you to
share the meaning of your calls so
        high and far away
I could see the earth unfold below me
        in calm mosaic to the curved horizon
know such strange connection
such unity of mind!
the half-forgotten dream
still draws my eyes
        remote and far away

how would it be if I had wings
would I lose at last the fear of change

Sandra Detweiler
Eugene, Oregon

Makeshift Borders

weigh it which way,
boundaries are cuffed barrels tongued to a busy road,
oil & hate trickling down to receive migrants in a befitting green.
you would almost beg to carry the whole fun below your chin.

at the steep edge, nature knows a little about slave trade.
she lays in blocks,
to break the world into a foreign queue.

rip off those lies in sack clothing,
& the shady officers—blond mannequins making reckless gains in
    cheap currency.
what makes you feel the snow kills better over there?
how come you've lost so much weight in chasing a life that is yours?

sweet-tongue me into your grief,
how you bear this lesson for someone out there with a brown skin,
about to cross a border that is no border.

tell him the truth that is no truth.
that an eruption quaked this land to meet us at both ends.
make a folklore of this, & watch variety stalk the most of its
    meaning.

Sophia Ashley (she/they)
Ikorodu, Lagos

The Seven Wonders of the World

There is a great unspooling of the mind
When the world, akimbo, tips down to the side
And the stars unravel to soften the fall
Of our dreams trickling down, hushed eyed

And weary. The seven hearted never tarried
Sin-swollen, lust faced, gluttony deluged
The slothful will never tread, the wrathful left for dead
Pride consumes in small phases, disillusioned

Jaded green as the greed seething foam from the seas
The waves lap like a tongue at the bowl
Envy twines amidst vines, canopied 'cross the sky
Tangled tracks bring down sun, bring down fowl

Life as we knew it, strung out, wave goodbye
The world untethers, snaps, and breaks
And we waited and cried, eager only for why
We had slept at the wheel, the world veering, awake

Ambrielle Butler (she/her)
El Lago, Texas

Morning Walks

We loved our morning walks—
the dogs and I—along
the red sandstone paths
in the foothills of the Rockies
to the outcropping of rocks
scalloped like the humpback
of a dinosaur, Horsetooth Reservoir
stretching below us. Some cactus.
Cows wandering, their rusty bells rattling.
Sometimes the hiss of colored
hot air balloons rising
over the next hill startled us.
We'd return home
red-dust-covered head to foot.
Not in any hurry to shake it off.

Bonny Barry Sanders
Jacksonville, Florida

For a Writer

For a helpless bag of stored up tears, I sure do act
like a brick wall. Trying not to make a fuss in public,
saves up the fuss for somewhere. A wasp under the eves
or in a jar is a wasp that does not die from stinging.

I don't have anything new to say and nothing I have ever
said has made a lick of difference. Is being unobtrusive
a resume-worthy skill? I am so naturally quiet
people back into me all the time. That must count

for something. I have no more time to write this. I have
to watch TV then sleep under piles of heavy blankets.
I have to rub my fingerprints from the bottles in your medicine
cabinet and sleep. This paper full of nonsense will outlast me.

Anne Rieman
Glendale, California

Baby's Big Book of Mommy

CHAPTER ONE: Babymommybaby.
        CHAPTER TWO: "Oh-oh, mommy's gone.
but hold on, wait…mommy's back! Yay-slurp-yay!"

        CHAPTER THREE: Mommy goes away.
"Again?" says baby, enduring the question,
        What is an *I*, & am I one?

Mommy returns. Then comes the dreaded
        CHAPTER FOUR in which "I have a life
not-mommy," says mommy. "Sorry about that."

        "Whaa?" says baby. "That makes no sense;
what if I don't want to be a person & die?"
        Skip ahead to CHAPTER SIX: Baby goes away.

"Whaa?" says mommy. "That makes no sense,"
        paving the way for the much-celebrated but often
                misunderstood
CHAPTER SEVEN wherein, *Distance is the bread*;

        baby writes in journal, *time alone the wine*,
& phones home saying, "Hey, mommy, it's me, baby.
        Check this out!" Silence. Mommy doesn't know

what to say. CHAPTER EIGHT in which
        baby takes a selfie, looks & sees a mommy
inside a baby inside a mommy,

        & asserts, "A mommy is a baby
in a mommy suit."
        Earns a PhD Comparative Lit.

Drunk one night (CHAPTER NINE) and feeling guilty,
        baby calls mommy. It's late
to be calling, and no one picks up.

Baby tries later. Still no answer.
Mommy? [Silence] No more means no more,
		baby recalls, the best books all say,

& flies home to look through mommy's desk drawers.
		Twinkle, twinkle, little star,
a toy piano plays—in CHAPTER TEN—

		how I wonder what you are. "Were," corrects baby,
enduring the question, What is an I, & am I one?
		alone in the presence of mommy.

Murray Silverstein
Oakland, California

The Looming After, and the Afterwards

i expected a ghost   like an animal twinned by taxidermy

   but what's gone   will never meet replacement

door i opened   & closed for days

   i can't control you any more   than you control me

winter candles the ghost   light as a planchette

   one communion of moths   levitating above the next

i couldn't sleep at night   afraid yet wanting her to visit to show

   herself to me clear as the prosthetic   sheen on a bell pepper

the loom is opening my seams   drizzling baby spiders like pierced
   yolks

   she doesn't need to convince me she's here   i'll reach into the
   dark anyways

Courtney Kalmbach
Pinckney, Michigan

Eric's House

You can be evicted from
the corpse of a house
as quickly as you can be evicted
from the shelter of a body.

> You smash the glass
> door in the den, just for fun, leaving
> a frame to slide
> on the track,
> no barrier between
> cold worlds.

You sleep in the open room,
glass shivering in the loops of the carpet,

> break through to nothing
> but belongings,
> boxed and naked shock.

Flowers that smell like carrion
and expose their rotting blooms
to the humidified air
remind me of you.

Slugged through to the beams,
gaping drywall tells the hollow
way of hunger: the plant with no
stems, leaves, or roots.

Here come the creatures, with their bottles
of sweet vermouth. Here come the pollinators.

Annabelle Bonebrake
Los Angeles, California

Box Boat Hot Spring

Sail away in a sieve I tell
myself, tits deep in a barrel

lodged along the banks of
the Middle Fork. Some kind

April stars concur, plunge
into unseen Sawtooths. You

regulate the temperature with
red buckets full of river water.

I don't mind the rotting smell.
I can't see the rusty bolts. I am

spinning and nude except
for a headlamp. The best

part of an adventure is not
knowing when you're on one.

Maura Way
Greensboro, North Carolina

After Reading Margaret Levine

I forget poetry
and go to my porch
that needs swept
of crimson maple leaves.

These last ones languish
though still pert in their middles,
with water the tree gave up
without discrimination
the entire bloated spring.

All day, the adventuresome
have leapt from branch ledges
to bathe briefly in afternoon sunlight,
then land here on the gray slab,
leaving a wet print of dark inky veins.

Dave Malone
West Plains, Missouri

Untact

These were once
my keywords:
dactylic hexameter
epic poetry
Homeric heroes
word cadences
lost pitch of song.

And my precious digs?
Nausikaa, a princess
washing, singing
the river clean:
laughter matrilineal.

Now far gone are
those shining epithets,
patronymics too,
replaced by machines.
Today, editing, I find a new word
freshly flagged:
      untact [stet].

Coined in South Korea,
it evokes 'intact'—
a dream economy where
distance-workers, Covid-free,
keep pace with automation:
no touch, no share,
not breath, not smell, nor taste.
You can work from anywhere.

But as dirty laundry, plastics,
acronyms, all keep piling up
in swirling islands somewhere in the Pacific,
there's a vision of a new world
with more and more AI—artificial intelligence—
- ai, ai, ai, - how quickly we mourn loss.
Who will take in clothes and shrouds, fresh, sun-dried?

Estuaries, will they ever again be clean?
Who will greet the heroes coming home?
And Nausikaa? Who knew her name
meant all along: "the burner of ships"?

Carolyn Clark
Newfield, New York

Note to Self: Rules for Decision-Making

#1
Take single sheet of blue-striped loose-leaf.
Annotate edges with key decisions
for next ten years. Leave 3"x 4" blank space
dead center. Write return address on back,
fold into airplane, pull open the
window, snap that wrist & pop the plane
over the pedestrian walkway toward
the construction zone so the cross currents
catch and carry it floating over the
brownstones to nose dive into the river.
Hope some lonely MIT oarsperson
rescues and analyzes it via
computing algorithms hidden within
the sewer systems of the entire
continental US. Assume they will
return the calculations printed right
in the center with a laminated
reference key safely attached for easy
reading.

#2
If #1 doesn't work out—
well, ask some good questions.
The right questions, like,
"What would the 70-year-old
version of me think of that?"

If no 70-year-old version of you yet exists,
find that person, by age and genetics, as close as you can get
in this particular set of space-time constraints.
Listen closely as he offers nothing
original. Remember originality
and wisdom seldom attend the same functions.

Pay attention as he volleys questions
just hard enough to make you stretch to reach them:
lunging as you used to in the tennis matches

the two of you would have years ago.
He had that little wooden
racket from the seventies;
you the 19.99 new Dick Sporting's Goods model
and you both tried to make the bouncing yellow ball
echo up and down the court.

Whatever he will say today,
write it down to think about later.
But, mostly, investigate the cadence of his queries.
Geoposition your future
hairline from his features.
If you stay on those courts long enough,
by the time you get home,
(twenty years ago or today)
you may find a crumpled note
slipped beneath the door, the edges all faded.
In the center, written with whatever is the future's version
of a ballpoint pen, a two-word data analysis:
Good decision.

Sean Beckett
Watertown, Massachusetts

Father's Day

He doesn't come by his fate easily.
Alone, at dusk, he empties another
wineglass while fireflies send
their light to the moon.
Better to grab the reins of
the sun god's chariot than suffer
this unrequited love.
Text messages that remain
unanswered. The waiting
feels like a million tiny
papercuts.
The distant freeway hum
a long continuous sigh.
Navigating the bridge from
here to there seems to depend
on a roll of the dice.
Loneliness best served alone,
there's no place to gulp
the infectious laughs
of happy people, no easy way
to slip through the seam
between the past and everything else.

Bruce Gunther
Bay City, Michigan

The River Tells

The river tells us
everything we need to know
its winter edges build and thicken
only to melt by inches on a warm day
never to be seen in that form again
the banks themselves, disfigured by the next storm

the creek bridge where we cast for trout
ruined by the weathering seasons
the sandbars where we tent at night
are returned by morning to silt on the river floor
the beaver chop, the cooing loon
the river itself passes us too soon
even the sigh and gurgle of river's talk
rises and falls into the selfsame dark

this is all we need—the fleeting sound
the morphing banks
the shifting ground
all we need as a map for our own freckling skin
our blinking love
impossible to grasp or hold
as river's ever-turning flow

the river, too, has another shore
freedom is in crossing over
where nothing in the entire
field of being is hidden

David John Rosenheim
Pacifica, California

Inaccurate Histories

Maybe my great-grandparents didn't take a steamer trunk
And head to Ellis Island to eat pasta
With cockroaches in a four-story walk-up in Harlem with no air-
    conditioning
Maybe the only heaviness my great-grandmother had to carry
From the bus up the flights of stairs
Were her rubies and emeralds and diamonds and pearls
And not the groceries
Maybe my great-grandpa had a happy family with a mother and father
And he knew his real last name, wasn't dropped off on the doorstep of
    some family friend
Never to speak of that family again
Maybe he didn't run booze and cheat at cards or eat rats while
    imprisoned fighting another man's war

Maybe this is all a farce and I wasn't born in the middle of a swamp
With mafia at the corner of the streets
With the little white house and Ambrose's candy store
Maybe I was born into more

There were no bodies buried under the boardwalk boards
The beach was clean, the sand was white
Nobody contracted AIDS and died

I didn't grow up

I didn't grow up

I made this all up

There is no family straining against the nooses of their history
There is nothing leaking from the roof
There is nothing breaking.

Alise Versella
Lanoka Harbor, New Jersey

Having It Out with Mortality

We are passing into some new life,
our children old enough to sleep late,
too big to crawl into our bed.
I find myself with time enough
to get lost in the tangle of your black hair,
dotted with more gray than I've ever noticed,
only seen this closely on a Saturday morning.

And I should be thinking of this, of
being here, of the time we have.
But instead I think of how your head
won't always be on this pillow, how
your body will be gone, how one day
it will likely be just me muttering out loud
to myself, our children too big to fit in this house.

Which is a greater expression of gratitude—
knowing this truth or luxuriating in the cool press
of sheets, the touch of your hand against my breast,
your beard that troubles the bare skin of my neck?
I think of your father dead in his grave
in a cemetery that we will never visit,
dead at 77. I do the math.

Jennifer Judge
Dallas, Pennsylvania

Grandpa Worked in a Glidden Paint Factory for Over 30 Years

Martin Johnson Heade, "Newburyport Meadows," 1876–81

Say bucolic and see the neglected
child of bubonic and colicky.

It's not a pretty word. It's sickly.
It's its own throat-clearing. Is it COVID,

she wonders? No, it's just bucolic,
but still; yet, here it is in prose pairing

with this painting, saying what I can see
for myself: a massive scene of storm

and field and water and work. Heade's wetlands,
although partly shadowed are front and low,

marshy but mirroring the golden haystacks.
Is the storm stage left coming or going?

Despite the distant rain, light pronounces
work in the center of everything.

A valley of sorts—rock ledges and sloped
green keep us attending to the work

at hand. No sheep anywhere—the herdsmen
gone to another pasture, a previous

poem, maybe. The haystacks, like raindrops
or gumdrops, stand sentinel or symbolic

or just statuary. In the belly
of it all, the horse, almost small enough

to be mistaken for a smudge, waits
for the storm, or is glad to see it go.

Everything's so clean, sterile, washed
and renewed while the work keeps on.

The laborers too far away—just white
dots—to notice how their shirts can still be

so white after a day out in the fields
before or after a storm this size.

The soil seems inundated with Adam's
ale; I sure wouldn't call it dirty

water, not with all this bucolicky
beauty to absorb, to try to swallow.

Jacob Stratman
Siloam Springs, Arkansas

Before Light Shifts

When old friends get together
and new partners
in their lives sit at the table
and the food goes into gullets
and the wine keeps pouring
and a point is reached
where old memories emerge
and new partners smile and nod
as if they were enjoying these
long ago escapades
as if they were remembering things
they never experienced
and then a fresh bottle is opened
and the conversation
shifts to them and their thoughts
on life and the world
which lasts a quick round
before words drift back
to when old friends lived
a life new partners
would never understand
or want to   in fact.

Marc Swan
Freeport, Maine

Contact

Dark beard fraying from his mask
hair on his arms dimpled
in the bright cold, the barista
slides open the window

hands me my coffee.
He wraps his fingers
around just the top of the cup
to hold the line between us
so fingers don't graze.

As he makes change I conjure
a different century, the two of us
courtly dancers in a line,
his coiled wig, my gown curved
like a bell. We nod and curtsy,
a man and woman passing
on to other partners.

The window scrapes open.
Coins drop into my palm.

Wandajune Bishop-Towle
Andover, Massachusetts

Commercial Break, Third Quarter

And we're off on a drone-flight
above uncountable acres of wheat fields
a pick-up bouncing along a dusty road
Rhapsody Americana   then the route shifts
to a spoonful of hearty chicken stew
the carrots a vibrant orange   broth
like the interior of a crystal ball revealing
bank robbers hauling bags of loot   it looks
like they'll get away   but the credit card
they were planning to use for their getaway
car is overcharged   (and yes they too
seem to realize they should have considered
this before the heist)   the cops close in
on the leafy parking lot of a Walmart
as customers exit with shopping carts
full of vacuums and PlayStations
and oil-free multi-functional fryers
smiles on their faces   and on the faces
of the fans back at the stadium   home
team with the ball   first and goal to go

David Starkey
Santa Barbara, California

Something Keeps Happening

Something keeps happening
all the time, even in sleep,
here, in the milk-white distance
of a slow moon's fecund light.

Fluid figures move freely
in small and large spaces,
framed in by their own loss,
their wish to be noticed.

But there are times when everything
is shut and closed. Coloured circles
and spots of blue and morning-red
are engaged in a glorious dance.

You ask yourself, is it for this
I have lived all these years?
Is it for this I've been trying
to locate myself in the world?
These nameless, numberless figures?

All the while the heart has been
listening to itself. It whispers,
"No, you are too innocent to see
the hidden lie. You are not this."

And then you look the other way—
deeper, farther—as far as your mind can go.
There is this absence, this vacancy that
quietly shows, the silence that refuses
to define itself, the lightness of it all.

Bibhu Padhi
Orissa, India

A Blue Dragonfly

hovers above
the river's cold persistence,
and here

I am, a tourist
in proximity, somewhat fidgety,
a classic pest

in my home, far
from castle walls, dragons,
or rushing water.

My fingers
are like the four wings
of a majestic

Odonata, abuzz
on the home
keys. Next to the river-

side are wild
lilies, but our insect flew away
—too soon,

or just in time—
for another
dragonfly appeared,

so real
that it was, and is, the same
enchantment.

Dana Stamps, II.
Riverside, California

We Share Our Old Dog's Dream

Our little dog, a terrier mongrel we inherited
from our daughter, stretches herself in sleep, a still life
of pursuit, of speed, her sleek snout fearlessly forward
in dream world we cannot see, her front legs folded slightly,
as if clearing a barrier, her rear legs extended
to remind us how high she once leaped, how fast she once ran.
Now she practices rest. She has reached her dotage
as she reached her ball—before we did. She gives us now
a foretaste of what's to come for us. Let's see. We are
a bit more than four times her age, but in dog years
she could be our parent or grandparent. We watch her dream,
quivers of glory past, of things chased and caught or scared
in her sleeping eyes, the idea of bark in her throat and jaws.
In the analgesic slumber of age, she is free of pain
and young and swift and wholly dog and perfect still.
I put my fingers behind her ear, just there, and she pushes
her head into my palm and makes that low moan, that sound
that is closest she can come to declaration of love.

Cecil Morris
Roseville, California

Frost Country

From Breadloaf, I jog downhill towards town.
I pass Wayside: site of the cabin where Frost
spent summers writing poems. It's a stone's throw
from the Frost House on Frost Road. There,
a yellow bus unloads middle school kids,
happy to break from school. I imagine

the old poet's craggy head in the clouds.
Then I see a sign for the Frost Interpretive Trail.
I weave through the parking lot past a Camry
and a mini-van. On the trail poems on plaques
intersperse with verses carved in wood.

Caught between delight and wisdom, I hesitate
at the fork for "The Road Not Taken."
Then I realize, it's a loop!
It doesn't make any difference
which path you choose. You always end up
back in the parking lot
with the Camry or the mini-van!

Well, I have to get back for lunch.
No stopping by woods for me.
I'm hungry and earth
is the right place for lunch.

Ed Meek
Somerville, Massachusetts

Arc de Ciel

Aretha sang R E S P E C T
a word I imagine in the sky in a

rainbow looking down over a flock
of blue herons flying near the Central

Expressway, near the train station
far away from the blue-brocade sofa I

upholstered to calm him, to soak up his
words *lazy, liar, slacker, bitch* his blows

to bend me, to extinguish me, until I see

                    an arc in the sky.

Joan Canby
Garland, Texas

Spring Melt

It's grey.
I'm nearly forty-nine,
which is nearly fifty.
We all know what that means.
Well, less than it used to
but more than we care to admit.
The plumbing slows.
Hope might just prove yet,
although I hope not,
that it springs forth
from a finite spring.
It's spring. It's been spring.
It will be spring
for four more months.
It's Canada in the north.
I turn off the blinking pages
of work. Poor reception.
Abandon my wallet.
Screw the government
and its progress reports.
I hunch to enter
my mind's back room.
All I ever wanted
was to read and reread
the books I read
to my children.
The same books
my dead parents
read to me.

Erin Wilson
Massey, Ontario, Canada

www.ingramcontent.com/pod-product-compliance
Lightning Source LLC
Chambersburg PA
CBHW031412310726
48971CB00003B/841